PRIMARY SOURCES OF POLITICAL SYSTEMS™

COLONIALISM
A PRIMARY SOURCE ANALYSIS

PHILIP WOLNY

rosen central
Primary Source™

The Rosen Publishing Group, Inc., New York

Published in 2005 by The Rosen Publishing Group, Inc.
29 East 21st Street, New York, NY 10010

Library of Congress Cataloging-in-Publication Data

Wolny, Philip.
Colonialism : a primary source analysis / Philip Wolny.— 1st ed.
    p. cm. — (Primary sources of political systems)
Includes bibliographical references and index.
Contents: The Spanish in the New World—The British in America—The British in India—The Dutch in South Africa—The French in Vietnam.
ISBN 0-8239-4516-2 (library binding)
1. Colonies—Juvenile literature. 2. Colonies—America—Juvenile literature. 3. Colonies—Asia—Juvenile literature. 4. Europe—Colonies—Juvenile literature. [1. Colonies. 2. World politics.]
I. Title. II. Series.
JV185.W65 2004
325'.3—dc22

2003015892

Manufactured in the United States of America

On the cover: England's Prince Edward *(left)* and the Begum (princess) of Bhopal *(second from left)* walking in a royal procession to Sadar Manzil Palace in Bhopal, India, in 1922.

CONTENTS

Introduction 5

Chapter One The Spanish in the New World 7

Chapter Two The British in America 14

Chapter Three The British in India 23

Chapter Four The Dutch in South Africa 34

Chapter Five The French in Vietnam 44

Timeline 55

Primary Source Transcriptions 57

Glossary 59

For More Information 60

For Further Reading 60

Bibliography 61

Primary Source Image List 62

Index 63

INTRODUCTION

The United States, born from thirteen British colonies, won its fight for independence more than 200 years ago. Other countries have struggled longer and harder for the right to self-determination and freedom.

"Colonialism" comes from the word "colony." A colony is usually a group of people living in a territory under the rule of a parent state. Almost always, a colony develops in a place where indigenous people have lived for generations with their own established culture and traditions. Sooner or later, the colonists and the indigenous people come into conflict.

Ancient people, such as the Greeks in the Mediterranean, the Persians in the Middle East, and the Huns in Mongolia, had colonies. They, and many groups throughout history, conquered and ruled their neighbors as well as peoples thousands of miles away. People living under foreign rule often struggle to maintain their cultures, their civil rights, and their resources.

The Age of Exploration brought the European powers to many parts of the world alien to them. It also brought them into contact with many people and nations. They

This illustration portrays Christopher Columbus claiming San Salvador for Spain shortly after landing there in 1492. Columbus was not the first European to reach the Americas. However, reports of his voyage made him famous for having "discovered" the New World.

eventually incorporated these peoples and their governments into their own empires. By the eighteenth century, the British were establishing control in India, the Dutch had a strong presence in South Africa, and the French had taken over Indochina, the area now made up of Laos, Cambodia, Vietnam, and Thailand.

Colonies share at least two features. Colonizers establish power over less powerful people, and they take more from the people than they give in return.

Up until the early part of the twentieth century, European nations controlled much of the earth's surface. The changes they made in the political and cultural landscape of the world, for good or ill, remain to this day.

CHAPTER ONE

THE SPANISH IN THE NEW WORLD

The first wave of modern European colonialism began after explorers reached the New World. The New World included the continents that are known today as North and South America, as well as the islands of the Caribbean. In 1492, Christopher Columbus claimed for Spain the island of Hispaniola (divided today into the Dominican Republic and the Republic of Haiti). Soon, the Spanish explored, conquered, and colonized many Caribbean islands and neighboring regions.

The Spanish explorers were often military men and adventurers. They were also known as "conquistadores," or conquerors.

Francisco Pizarro first sailed to the New World in 1509. He took part in a number of Spanish explorations before he conquered the Incan Empire in 1532.

The conquistadores defeated the native people they encountered again and again despite being outnumbered, sometimes by more than a hundred to one. They had superior weapons, including firearms, which native people had never seen. But the Europeans also exposed the indigenous people to deadly diseases. In a terrifyingly short time, people of ancient cultures had been nearly wiped out by illness.

The Incas

One of the native groups the conquistadores came upon, and eventually conquered, were the Incas. At the time, the Incas had an advanced and extensive empire. Based in present-day Peru, the empire extended nearly 2,500 miles (4,023 kilometers) along the western coast of South America. The Spanish crown sent conquistador Francisco Pizarro to claim for Spain the land south of Panama along the western coast. In 1531, with a force of 180 men, Pizarro easily captured the Incan king Atahuallpa, who had 30,000 Incan warriors at his command. The Spanish eventually executed Atahuallpa in 1533. Subduing the Incas with advanced weapons, the Spanish spent the next few years cementing their hold, as they removed the riches of the Incan Empire.

The Spanish and the Church

Once Spain controlled Mexico, large parts of South America, and the West Indies by the mid-1500s, the stage was set for the first wave of European colonialism. Spain and Portugal wanted these lands that were thought to be rich in gold and silver. Both nations were

One of the greatest early victories of the Spanish conquistadores was the defeat of the Incan ruler Atahuallpa. This engraving from 1595 depicts the strangulation of Atahuallpa, who is seated to the left, by Francisco Pizarro's soldiers. The death of the last Incan king marked the end of the Incan Empire.

heavily influenced by the Roman Catholic Church, which was a major political force in Europe at the time. The church decided to divide the known lands between the two countries.

The Inter Caetera

In 1493, Pope Alexander VI issued the Inter Caetera. This papal bull, or decree of the church, was written at the request of King Ferdinand and Queen Isabella of Spain. It declared that the sacred mission of the explorers was to convert the native people to Catholicism. Most people living in the Americas, like the Incas and Aztecs, were polytheistic, which means that they worshiped many gods. The Spanish and Portuguese used the decree to justify conquering and controlling people who were not Christian. They considered indigenous people to be savages, inferior to Catholic Europeans. Because the Spanish and Portuguese thought that God approved their actions, they were all the more eager to proceed with their quest.

The Encomienda System

The Spanish devised a system to split up their new territories. It was called *encomienda*, meaning "charge" or "mission." It was based on the feudal system of land grants that existed in Spain at the time. A Spaniard arriving in the New World was issued land. As the *encomendero*, this man ruled over a certain number of Native Americans. The number depended on the size of the land granted to him by the Spanish crown.

Each encomendero was supposed to protect the Indians on his land. However, the Native Americans were required to pay a tribute, or tax, to the encomendero. The church also required the encomendero to convert his subjects to Christianity.

The system of encomienda was supposed to "improve" most of the Native Americans and "civilize" them. However, many encomenderos treated the Native Americans as subhuman slaves. They regarded them as a cheap source of labor.

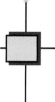

In addition, the Native Americans had no immunity to European diseases. Thousands died from illnesses carried by the Spanish. Also, whether on plantations or in the harsh environments of mines where they were forced to dig for precious metals, Indians were literally worked to death.

The Spanish invaders were killing off workers faster than they could be replaced. Administrators in the mother country, prodded by concerned missionaries, tried to reduce these abuses. With the great distance between Spain and the New World, it took a long time for instructions to reach the colonists. Many colonists disregarded these rules. Often, people sent over to ensure that Spain's rules were followed became part of the problem themselves.

The New Laws

King Charles I of Spain passed the New Laws of 1542 to abolish the enslavement of Native Americans. As a result, the encomenderos turned to the African slave trade to supply their labor source.

The New Laws established a number of reforms. No more encomiendas would be granted. Spanish settlers who abused the slaves in their stations could lose their encomiendas. Encomiendas could no longer be passed down from father to son. When an encomendero died, power over his encomienda returned to the Spanish king.

The Spanish also set up the *audiencia*, a colonial government that would answer directly to the king and queen. Only members of the audiencia were allowed to distribute land. These new measures sought to rein in Spanish settlers who were especially brutal.

THE INCAS BEFORE THE SPANISH

Before the arrival of the Spanish, the Incas in Peru lived under a class system similar to many European societies. The Incan system was split into three parts. A small ruling class made the decisions for everyone. Below the rulers was a class of aristocrats. The third and lowest class was the laborers.

The Incas were reported to have had a social welfare system. Under this system, old and injured workers were provided an income after they became unable to work. However, the rule of law in Incan society was also very strict. Under Incan law, a seemingly minor crime such as theft often carried a penalty of death.

This painting, created sometime in the late eighteenth century, depicts the dynasty of former Incan rulers. It was salvaged from a Peruvian school of that era.

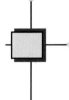

A Revolt Against the Crown

In Peru, the center of New Spain—the name for Spanish lands in the Western Hemisphere—the encomenderos were particularly worried about these laws. In 1841, Francisco Pizarro, who conquered Peru, was killed during a property dispute between Spanish landholders. One of his brothers, Gonzalo Pizarro, led a revolt of landholders against the new administration.

In the end, the Spanish suspended the New Laws. The rebellion had cut off the flow of riches from New Spain to the mother country. King Charles I sent Pedro de la Gasca as an emissary, or representative, to regain the support of the settlers.

De la Gasca met Gonzalo Pizarro in battle. On April 9, 1548, Pizarro and his followers were defeated, and Pizarro was executed.

While the rule of the crown was reestablished, the encomienda system never really disappeared. In fact, many of those charged with getting rid of its worst abuses were themselves encomenderos. Some of them were cruel, while others took care of the Indians they ruled over. Spanish settlers eventually rebelled against the crown.

Times were changing. Other nations would enter the race for economic world dominance. In the coming centuries, British and other European powers would hold sway over much of the earth's surface and forever change the lives of millions of people. By the early half of the nineteenth century, Spain had lost all of its colonies in the Western Hemisphere, except for Cuba.

CHAPTER TWO

THE BRITISH IN AMERICA

British settlers moved to North America to find a place where they could worship as they chose and search for economic opportunity. But the vast continent, which was part of what they called the New World, wasn't empty. Native Americans had lived there for thousands of years. Nevertheless, the settlers considered it their right to take over and govern the land. The ensuing battle between the new arrivals and the Native Americans shaped the future of the new American nation as it destroyed ancient civilizations. The institution of slavery, established by the British colonists first in Virginia, would also create great upheaval.

George Washington was the leader of the Continental army against Britain during the American Revolution. Earlier, he had fought valiantly for Britain during its war against France for control over North American territories.

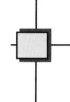

New Arrivals

The first permanent British settlement in North America was Jamestown. Founded on May 14, 1607, on the coast of present-day Virginia, Jamestown struggled to exist right from the beginning. Starvation, illness, and bitter cold during the winter of 1610 reduced the original group of 500 people to about sixty.

By 1617, the settlers had learned how to grow corn and tobacco. But there weren't enough people to farm effectively. In 1619, Jamestown settlers brought in indentured servants from Europe and Africa. The servants would earn their freedom after four to seven years of labor. Forty years later, Jamestown became the first American colony to create laws legalizing slavery.

As the British colonists pushed farther into the wilderness around Jamestown, they fought the Indians who inhabited these lands. Over time, Jamestown became the home of the wealthier members of the colony, while the frontier was inhabited by new, poor arrivals. It was mostly these newcomers who fought the Indians and suffered the most from their counterattacks.

The Conquest of New England

North of Virginia, in present-day Massachusetts, a group of Puritan settlers landed at Plymouth Rock. They established the Plymouth colony in 1620. These colonists were known as the Pilgrims. They were members of a religious sect that was very strict in its beliefs and had fled Britain to escape persecution from the Church of England.

This undated illustration from the nineteenth century shows Pilgrims landing at Plymouth Rock in Plymouth, Massachusetts, in 1620. The man standing in the middle appears to be greeting someone, perhaps even one of the Native Americans the Pilgrims encountered upon their arrival.

The Pequot Indians, who had long inhabited the area that was to become Massachusetts, survived off the land, in harmony with nature. The new settlers wanted to clear the forests to make the land suitable for farming.

Pilgrim v. Pequot

The Pilgrims and the Pequot Indians coexisted for a time. However, the Pilgrims started a war with the Pequot in 1636 over the death of a Pilgrim fur trader who was killed by the Pequot. There were massacres on both sides. The Pilgrims often killed Pequot women and children during raids. They justified this with their belief that the Pequot were savages who had not accepted the Christian religion and were, as a result, doomed to damnation. Many times, the Pequot counterattacks were equally ferocious. The Pilgrims used their advanced firepower to overwhelm the Pequot.

Pequot Indian leaders sent this petition to Governor Joseph Talcott of Connecticut in 1735, asking him to end colonial invasion of their tribal lands. Refer to page 57 for a transcription.

From 1675 to 1676, the colonists fought another Native American tribe, the Wampanoag. The British colonists accused Metacom, the Wampanoag chief, of murder. Most colonists didn't seem to want this conflict, but leaders of the Plymouth colony were set on taking new lands from the Indians. This bloody war claimed the lives of hundreds of settlers and 3,000 Wampanoag, including Metacom.

THE IROQUOIS AND THE COLONIAL ERA

Well before the Europeans arrived in the Western Hemisphere, the Native Americans of what is now northern New York State had organized themselves into a single nation known as the Iroquois League. By 1722, the Cayuga, Onondaga, Oneida, Mohawk, Seneca, and Tuscarora were part of an efficient political body. Clan and village chiefs sat in councils in which every tribe had a vote.

The Iroquois fought neighboring tribes as well as the settlers of New France (in the territories north of New York, now part of Canada). They kept an uneasy peace with the British in northern New York because they traded with them.

When the thirteen colonies rebelled against the British, the league's loyalties were split. Some Indians sympathized with the British because they had gone much further than the colonists in guaranteeing them their lands.

The Oneida and Tuscarora tribes fell in with the colonists. The others attacked American settlements on the frontier. In 1779, an expedition of 4,000 American troops defeated the remaining Iroquois near Elmira, New York.

The decline of the Iroquois was ushered in by two treaties. The first Treaty of Fort Stanwix was signed in 1768. The second Treaty of Fort Stanwix was signed in 1784. Each gave white settlers vast expanses of land from New York down to what is now Tennessee. Masses of white people began moving onto the lands, much of which was in dispute between the Iroquois and other tribes. The stage was set for Americans to expand westward.

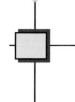

Armed conflict with the colonists was not the only peril for Native Americans during this era. Smallpox and other diseases to which they had no natural immunity took a terrible toll. For example, about 3,000 Wampanoag lived on the island of Martha's Vineyard in 1642, when the British settled there. A short time later, only about 300 Wampanoag had survived. Their population had been ravaged by smallpox.

The American Colonies and the Slave Trade

Another group that suffered from the colonial expansion in the New World was Africans. Kidnapped from their homes and brought to America as slaves, Africans were forced to perform menial labor and live under harsh, inhuman conditions.

The first African slaves arrived in Jamestown, Virginia, in 1619. They were used to cultivate tobacco in the mid-Atlantic colonies, especially around Chesapeake Bay.

Bacon's Rebellion

One of the greatest fears of wealthy and powerful colonists was that lower-class whites would join with black slaves in revolt. This became a reality in 1676. One of the causes of Bacon's Rebellion, as this uprising was called, was the issue of Native American raids on white settlers.

Frontiersmen in western Virginia were constantly battling the Native Americans. They usually received little help from the aristocracy in Jamestown. The governing body of Virginia, the House of Burgesses, did little to protect them. One landowner, Nathaniel Bacon, who had fought Native Americans himself, was elected to the house in 1676. He hoped to convince Virginians to declare total war on the Native Americans. When he didn't get help, he declared that he would organize his own forces against the Native Americans.

Virginia's governor, William Berkeley, declared Bacon a rebel and had him imprisoned. Two thousand Virginians marched in Jamestown in support of Bacon. Berkeley released him under pressure of this protest. Bacon then gathered a militia of his supporters and waged attacks on the Native Americans. But he also was angry at the Jamestown government. He thought that its taxes were too high, its members were corrupt, and it was monopolizing trade. Bacon fought a militia rallied by Berkeley. At one point, Bacon and his group controlled much of Virginia.

The Virginians who followed Bacon were mainly disgruntled frontier farmers, servants, and other people who were struggling to make a living. Many of them had been badly affected by the failures of the corn and tobacco crops that year. Also, they resented the power of the Jamestown elite.

In one of the last battles of the conflict, a ship on the York River forced the surrender of 400 men. Among these were blacks and whites, both slaves and servants. Poor whites who had immigrated to America as indentured servants were among the poorest of the lower class in their native England. The rebellion was finally put down after Bacon died of an unknown illness at the age of twenty-nine in the fall of 1676.

Black and White

Slavery grew steadily as the plantation system prospered. In 1661, a law was passed in Virginia that forbade blacks and whites from associating with each other as they had been doing in the colony for some time. In 1700, there were about 6,000 slaves living in Virginia. Slaves comprised less than 10 percent of the population. Within seventy years, slaves in Virginia numbered as many as 170,000, half of the state's population.

Slave Rebellion

By the late eighteenth century, many slaves rebelled. Some refused to do certain kinds of work, while others attempted escapes or plotted against their owners. Some newly arrived slaves from Africa ran off and formed their own communities on the frontier, where the English feared to go. Some escaped slaves found sympathy among the Native Americans who were enemies of the colonists. Some even intermarried and became part of Native American tribes.

In response, many of the colonial leaders set up severe penalties for slave disobedience. Punishment included whipping, branding, torture, and often death. Punishment was made harsh to discourage attempts at escape. For example, in 1705, Virginia declared that escaped slaves could be punished by dismemberment. Maryland passed a law in 1723 that punished slaves by cutting off their ears if they attacked their masters. Despite these cruel and frightening laws, in the mid-eighteenth century, landowners and other white colonists continued to fear slave revolts.

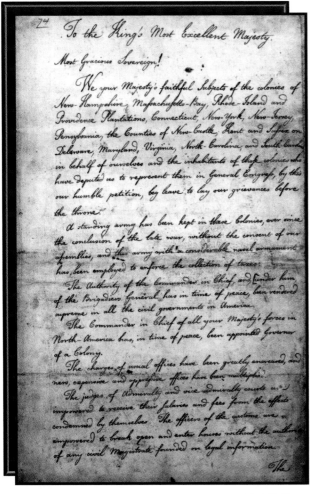

On July 5, 1775, the Continental Congress sent the Olive Branch Petition to King George III of England. It was a final attempt to find a peaceful solution to the colonies' dispute with England. King George refused to accept the petition. Refer to page 57 for a partial transcription.

America on the Road to Independence

The thirteen American colonies would eventually join together as a new nation. But only through the work of slaves and poor settlers did the colonies eventually become strong enough for independence. In their drive to survive and expand, the British settlers enslaved hundreds of thousand of Africans and destroyed Native American lives.

By 1776, the colonies no longer wanted Britain to set their policies. Many people in the newer generation of colonists saw England as a foreign power seeking to control them. The seeds had been planted for a break from England and the formation of a new nation. But even after America's independence through the American Revolution, the unrest among whites, blacks, and Native Americans would continue to shape the new nation for generations to come.

CHAPTER THREE

THE BRITISH IN INDIA

By the eighteenth century, the Industrial Revolution was changing the meaning of power in the Western world. For the conquerors of previous eras, the aim had been to amass riches such as gold and silver. But wealth after the Industrial Revolution was acquired by selling natural resources and manufactured goods. The people making these goods needed more places to sell them. Their home markets just weren't big enough.

The Industrial Revolution also required more raw materials to use in manufacturing as well as more food to feed the growing European population. Colonies would provide for these needs.

Queen Victoria of England assumed the title of empress of India in 1877. However, she never visited the country, which was easily England's most important colonial possession.

The East India Company

In 1600, Queen Elizabeth granted a charter (a license to operate) to the East India Company. It would run Britain's trade with Asia. Over the next few decades, the company set up trading ports along the coast of India.

For much of the 1600s, India was ruled by to the Mughals, a Muslim minority that ruled a large Hindu majority. In 1627, the Mughal emperor Jahangir gave the East India Company permission to build a factory at Surat, the Mughals' most important port city.

The East India Company also set up a military branch to protect its interests. British communities formed in the major cities of Bombay, Calcutta, and Madras. As the Mughals lost influence, the British were poised to grab it. They got their chance in 1856 in Bengal.

The Black Hole of Calcutta

A nawab was an aristocratic Indian ruler who headed an Indian principality, or region. In 1756, Nawab Siraj-ud-Dawlah took over Fort William and Calcutta, which were controlled by the British East India Company. At the time, it was reported that Nawab Siraj-ud-Dawlah had imprisoned more than 100 Englishmen in an airless jail cell in Fort William and that they had all died overnight. Although the story may have been greatly exaggerated (or never happened at all), the British believed it was true. Known as the Black Hole of Calcutta incident, it was considered an act of war.

The British were led by Robert Clive, a former civil service member who had become a military commander. They defeated

This painting depicts the ceremony in which Shah Alum, the Mughal emperor of India, shown seated on an elevated throne, transfers financial administration of the Bengali, Behar, and Orissa principalities to the British. Robert Clive, the British governor of India, is shown receiving the decree from the emperor as Indian and British officials look on.

Nawab Siraj-ud-Dawlah, in large part by bribing his troops. The nawab's body was found in a nearby river days after the battle.

Now Bengal, an important and wealthy Indian state, was under the control of the East India Company. Through a mixture of violence, more bribery, and clever negotiation, the East India Company would slowly reshape India.

A New Era Dawns

Over the next few years, Robert Clive's government in Bengal was marked by great corruption. He also convinced the emperor that the East India Company should collect the taxes in Bengal as well as in the province of Bihar.

In response to corruption in Bengal, the British Parliament passed the Regulating Act of 1773. This placed a governor-general in Bengal who answered to Parliament instead of to the East India Company. A supreme court was set up to regulate the affairs of the British in India. However, grave abuses by the court, including harsh penalties for minor crimes in the city of Calcutta, spread resentment among the colonized people.

Consolidation

The British underwent a period of annexation, acquiring states as buffers between their land and potential enemies. Later, they took land for the sake of power.

Between 1797 and 1805, Lord Richard Colley Wellesley, a governor-general, introduced the subsidiary system. Under it, the British would offer to protect a weaker neighbor against its stronger enemies. In exchange, the state would pay for the cost of the British army or give some of its land to the British.

In 1784, British prime minister William Pitt signed the India Act. It required that the East India Company answer to a Board of Control ruled by the British crown. Governor-generals could now be removed by the mother country.

This political cartoon, created by James Gillray in 1809, satirizes the insatiable appetite for world power shared by British prime minister William Pitt *(left)* and French emperor Napoléon Bonaparte. The caption reads "The Plumb Pudding in Danger . . . or, the State Epicures taking un Petit Souper [a Little Supper], the great Globe itself and all which it inherit."

Political Changes

Lord Charles Cornwallis became governor-general of British India in 1786. Cornwallis banned private trade among the employees of the East India Company and enforced a more rigid code of discipline. Indian high officials were replaced by British citizens. The introduction of British law also created confusion, since most Indians did not understand the British court system.

Under Cornwallis, tax and land administration were radically reformed. In Bengal, prior to British rule, a group of people called the zamindars had collected land revenue for imperial officials. The zamindars kept one-tenth of the land in exchange for their services. Many of their posts had been hereditary, passed along from father to son for generations.

Zamindars had maintained law and order. Also, they had supplied troops in times of conflict. Cornwallis's reforms were established in a new law called the Permanent Settlement of Bengal. Before, the land did not really belong to the zamindars. However the law made the zamindars into landowners, much like landlords in Britain.

Within a few years, many of the original zamindars were gone. They couldn't afford new taxes demanded by the British. They were replaced by entrepreneurs from faraway cities.

Resistance

Meanwhile, many Indians serving in Bengal's army under the British were angry. Since the British takeover, their wages had dropped. For decades, they lived in miserable conditions, often without proper sanitation or sewage. But an issue involving a new type of rifle was the last straw.

The Sepoy Rebellion

The British introduced a new rifle to their military in May 1857, in the city of Meerut, Bengal. The rifles' ammunition was packed in greased cartridges. To load this rifle, a person had to bite off the end of the cartridge.

This engraving is entitled *India: The Sepoy Rebellion, Repelling a Sortie Before Delhi*. In the battle that inspired the engraving, the British had fallen back and hidden to lull the sepoys into a false sense of security. Then the British launched a surprise attack that drove back the sepoys.

The gun makers had made a crucial cultural mistake. The material to be bitten off was made from a mixture of beef and pork. This greatly offended both Hindu and Muslim soldiers. Hindus consider cows sacred, while Muslims are not allowed to eat pork. Many of the outraged soldiers refused to accept the new cartridges and were chained for insubordination.

On May 10, 1857, fellow soldiers freed the captives. They escaped to nearby Delhi. More sepoys, Indian soldiers trained to serve under the British, joined them, and they claimed the city as theirs. They declared Bahadhur Shan II, the powerless Mughal emperor, their leader.

The British attempted to recall the cartridges and atone for their mistake. But it was too late. The combined British military in India, about 23,000 troops, found themselves facing a native Indian revolt comprised of about 300,000 people. This revolt was known as the Sepoy Rebellion. It was one of the bloodiest and most shocking of all colonial wars. Both sides committed atrocities.

The British were initially outnumbered, but reinforcements and the support of other Indians helped the British turn the tide of battle. Though their passion for freedom ran deep, the rebels were disorganized. They had no aim other than to punish the British. The highly organized British took Delhi back on September 20, 1857. The British reclaimed India.

The East India Company was blamed for the revolt. Its power was transferred directly to the British crown. The era of the East India Company was over.

The Road to Independence

Almost three decades later, the first seeds of Indian independence were planted in December 1885, with the first meeting of the Indian National Congress (INC). It was attended by lawyers and Indian professionals who wanted a greater voice in the rule of their country. In 1906, the Muslim League was founded for much the same reason.

One of the most notable features of the independence movement was nonviolent resistance. It became an effective tool for the INC and its middle-class professionals. For example, Lord George N. Curzon attempted to split up Bengal in 1905. One side would have a Muslim majority. The other side would be mainly Hindu. The INC denounced the move as an attempt to "divide and conquer" the people of Bengal.

Protest spread throughout India, as the INC and other groups urged millions of people to use nonviolent resistance. Hindus in Bengal boycotted British goods and burned cloth products from Lancashire,

This 1895 photograph shows Lord Curzon (1859–1925) in full ceremonial dress. Curzon was the viceroy of India from 1898 to 1905. It was in the last year of his reign that his attempt to divide Bengal into separate Muslim and Hindu states sparked widespread unrest throughout India.

England. Many Indians promised to wear only traditional native-made clothing. This protest extended to products such as those made of glass and metal. It helped reinvigorate local industry. Many people in India found great solidarity in this kind of protest.

GANDHI AND NONVIOLENCE

One of the greatest heroes in India's struggle against British colonialism was Mohandas Gandhi (1869–1948). A spiritual man and a pacifist, Gandhi promoted peace between Hindus, Muslims, and other Indian groups.

Gandhi's philosophy was rooted in nonviolence. He believed in a concept called *satyagraha*, meaning "the devotion to truth." It required people to strive against wrongs in a nonviolent way, no matter what the cost. This included protesting through fasting and civil disobedience, and accepting whatever repercussions were to come. Using nonviolence, resisters would make the oppressors, especially the violent ones, change their ways, and create understanding between both parties.

Through Gandhi's efforts, the movement for Indian independence swelled. His commitment to nonviolence in the face of considerable harassment from colonial officials proved a powerful example for the colonized Indians. Thousands of protestors performed peaceful sit-ins, blockades, and boycotts to flood the prisons and provoke rulers. World opinion was often strongly against the British, who were perceived as barbaric in their repression of nonviolent protests.

The British viceroy of India, Lord Louis Mountbatten, declares Indian independence on August 15, 1947, in New Delhi. Despite this newfound freedom and calls for restraint from leaders such as Gandhi, Muslims and Hindus would clash violently in the ensuing months over the partition of India into India and Pakistan.

The Partition of India

After World War II, the dream of Indian independence became reality. At first the results were horrifying. The division of India into a majority-Hindu state (India proper) and a majority-Muslim state (Pakistan) created unprecedented violence in 1947. As millions of people migrated from one area to the other, clashes between the groups left hundreds of thousands dead. Two nations were now free to pick up the pieces of hundreds of years of colonialism.

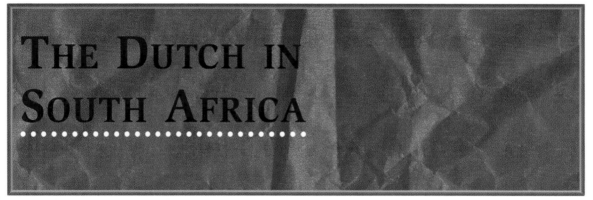

CHAPTER FOUR

THE DUTCH IN SOUTH AFRICA

The European takeover of South Africa started early in the seventeenth century. That is when the Dutch East India Company created settlements off the Cape of Good Hope, the southernmost tip of the African continent. Dutch men who had worked for the company were released from their contracts in 1657. They began settling the land in the immediate area.

The Dutch Meet the Africans

At first the Africans traded with their new Dutch visitors. The Africans included the Khoikhoi and the San, groups of indigenous herders, hunters, and gatherers.

Baron Horatio Kitchener led the British military campaign against the Boers in the Boer War in South Africa. He also served in various colonial positions in Sudan and Egypt.

However, they soon came into conflict. The Dutch kept slaves and thought themselves superior to the indigenous peoples. They fought the Khoikhoi, pushing them farther inland. Africans also perished from smallpox, which the Europeans had carried with them.

The Dutch often killed the African men and enslaved the women and children. By 1800, the Dutch controlled the western edge of what is today South Africa.

A Clash of Cultures

A group of settlers who had left Cape Town to move into the frontier called themselves the Trekboers, or "wandering farmers." They lived a strict, bare existence. By the late eighteenth century, the Trekboers, or, simply, the Boers, were quickly conquering their African neighbors. They were staunch Calvinists, Christians similar to the Puritans who first colonized New England. Like colonists before and after them, the Boers considered it their divine mandate to defeat non-Christians and to tame the wilderness.

The Boers expanded into lands occupied by the Xhosa (pronounced KOH-sa) peoples, whom they fought bitterly. The Boers developed a commando system, in which small bands of guerilla fighters would strike wherever they were needed.

The Khoikhoi, living closer to Cape Town, were controlled by the Dutch who treated them harshly. A Khoikhoi who attacked a white person would be put to death by being impaled on a spear. The Dutch were so contemptuous of "colored" people that they even denied descendants of Dutch-African marriages citizenship rights.

The British Takeover

In 1795, the British invaded the Cape region. They gained possession of the Cape Colony in 1806. This was an important acquisition for Britain because of the Cape's value as a trading link to the Near and Far East.

The British brought more colonists, many of them arriving in 1820. This strained the already tense situation between the Africans and the Europeans. To ease tensions between the already established Boers and new British colonists, and to gain more territory, the British launched fierce attacks on neighboring Africans.

The Great Trek

The Boers at first tolerated British rule. But, like American frontiersmen, they sought new lands of their own. They also left British-ruled areas because they favored slavery, which the British had outlawed in 1838.

Between 1835 and 1843, about 12,000 Boers left the main British-administered territory. This became known as the Great Trek. They took over land using their superior weapons and by making military pacts with the powerful tribes they encountered. Whenever the British attempted to interfere in affairs between the Boers and the independent natives on this northern frontier, it led to more bloodshed. The British withdrew for a time and granted independence to the two new Boer states that had been established, Transvaal and the Orange Free State.

Both Boer states instituted the strict regime of what later was known as apartheid. Meaning "apartness" in the Boers' language, Afrikaans, apartheid meant that whites and nonwhites were to be strictly segregated, or separated, in both church and state. This usually meant that the nonwhites lived under far worse conditions and oppression. This policy would last well into the 1980s.

The Boer War

The Boers and British expanded their power over their African neighbors. But the discovery of gold, diamonds, and other precious materials set the stage for eventual war between the two.

The discovery of diamonds on the frontier in 1867 brought min-

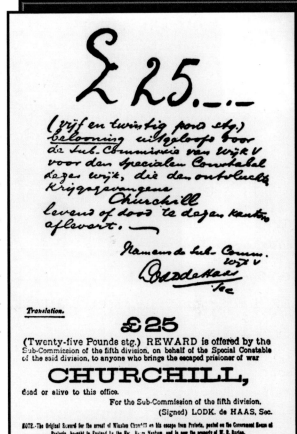

This wanted poster, created in 1899, offered a £25 reward (a small fortune at the time) for the capture or killing of Winston Churchill, a British news correspondent during the Boer War. He was captured by the Boers but escaped. Churchill went on to become prime minister of Great Britain (1940–1945, 1951–1955).

ing to northern South Africa. The British soon moved to annex the whole area as part of a British-controlled federation. By the end of the nineteenth century, a large group of mainly English settlers had

Soldiers rise from their battle positions during the Boer War in this photograph taken in 1901. Though the greatly outnumbered Boers did unexpectedly well, the superior British military eventually overwhelmed them.

come to Transvaal, now called the South African Republic. These were the Utlanders. The British wanted the Boers to grant political rights to these settlers, who had come to mine gold in the region.

The Boers of the South African Republic and the Orange Free State did not comply. On October 11, 1899, the Boers declared war on the British because the British had reinforced a military garrison (or base) and the Boers took this as a threat against them. Half a million British faced off against only 88,000 Boers.

Despite early Boer victories, the British gained the upper hand. One British general, Horatio Herbert Kitchener, made a ruthless bid to crush the Boers. Kitchener's forces burned and pillaged Boer towns and villages, along with those of Africans. Thousands of Boers were placed in concentration camps, where more than 20,000 women and children perished. The Boer commandos, though scoring small and occasional victories, were eventually forced to surrender.

The Treaty of Vereeniging in 1902 ended the Boer War. The Boers were disarmed, and the British military took over the South African Republic and the Orange Free State. The British made one concession to the Boers, however. They agreed to delay voting rights for non-whites until after the Boers had established their own government. This sealed the fate of nonwhites in South Africa for decades.

The Fight Against Apartheid

The Union of South Africa was established on May 31, 1910 bringing together the entire region for the first time. Under the new constitution, nonwhites were given no power. Apartheid became the official system of the new society.

The population of the union was made up of the Boers, also known as Afrikaners, the British, the African majority, and various workers, such as Indians. Even in the more liberal territory of the Cape, only whites could hold political office. As of 1910, only 5 percent of the African population could vote.

Protesters voice their opposition to apartheid in South Africa during a march on the South Africa House in London, England, in 1956. Included are members of the Movement for Colonial Freedom and the Black Sash Movement, a women's antiapartheid group. Worldwide opposition was partly responsible for ending apartheid years later.

Over time, the Afrikaners' influence grew. Afrikaans became South Africa's official language in 1925, replacing Dutch.

Apartheid Tightens Its Noose

By 1931, the Statute of Westminster in the British Parliament gave full independence to South Africa. In the following years, whites increased

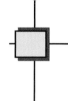

their power. The government provided money and other support to white farmers, with the aim of lifting all whites out of poverty. Blacks were prevented from holding better jobs. In 1936, the few nonwhites with voting rights had them taken away by Parliament. The standard of living jumped for whites as South Africa became an economic power at the end of the 1930s. It stayed the same or worsened for nonwhites, which included Africans and a large Indian population.

Africans Struggle for a Voice

In 1950, Parliament passed further laws to separate the people by color. The Population Registration Act classified every resident of the nation according to race. Interracial marriage or sexual relations were strictly prohibited. Africans could not go to the same hotels, movies, restaurants, or even funeral homes as whites. Police could also arrest and imprison blacks without trial or legal representation under laws enacted later. In 1951, the South African government set up the Natives Representatives Council to oversee "homelands" that grouped the Africans living in the countryside into separate areas. The chiefs of these homelands were often handpicked by the white government and were easily controlled by them.

By the 1970s, South Africa was among the most modern and wealthy nations on the continent. But whites, comprising one-fifth of the population, held great power over the nonwhites who provided most of the labor and services.

In response to apartheid, a new political movement sprang up among the African majority. This was the South African Native National Congress, which later became the African National

NELSON MANDELA: STRUGGLE AND SACRIFICE

Nelson Mandela is synonymous with the struggle against apartheid. Born the son of a chieftain of the Tembu people, Mandela gave up the chieftainship to earn a law degree in 1942. Within two years, he became a member of the ANC.

By 1949, Mandela had become a party leader. By the 1950s, the ANC was engaged in nonviolent antiapartheid campaigns.

In 1962, the ANC was banned and Mandela was sentenced to five years in prison. When weapons were discovered at a house associated with the ANC, Mandela admitted that he was involved. He was given a life sentence.

During his nearly thirty years in prison, Mandela inspired antiapartheid crusaders and rallied world opinion against South Africa. Many nations imposed economic sanctions on the country, while millions fought against apartheid from within. In the late 1980s, a new president, F. W. de Klerk, freed Mandela. Together they won the Nobel Peace Prize for their efforts to ease South Africa into an integrated democracy.

When South Africa held the first elections in which all people could vote, Mandela was elected president and the ANC became the majority party.

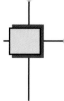

Congress (ANC). This group would play a major role in the struggle for black self-determination.

By the 1960s, the protest movement among the native Africans was growing. An African lawyer, Nelson Mandela, and other leaders provided the inspiration for protesters. The Pan-Africanist Congress (PAC), led by a university teacher named Robert Sobukwe, launched a protest in March 1960. During the protest, thousands subjected themselves to arrest by arriving at police stations without identification passes, which was against the law. At one demonstration near the city of Johannesburg, police fired into the crowds, killing sixty-seven people. Later they arrested up to 11,000 people.

The ANC and PAC soon changed their tactics and started committing violent acts such as bombing government buildings. Both Nelson Mandela and Robert Sobukwe were arrested by the government and sentenced to long prison terms. The ANC and other antiapartheid groups were banned.

Throughout the 1980s, political pressure from around the world and from within South Africa made real change possible. Mandela and other leaders, including Anglican archbishop Desmond Tutu, continued to speak out against apartheid. Large strikes and nonviolent protests forced the hand of the South African government. In 1989, F. W. de Klerk was elected leader of the ruling National Party and the country. Two years later, he announced a system of radical reforms: the repeal of many apartheid laws, a general political amnesty, and the freeing of Nelson Mandela on February 11, 1990.

In 1994, the ANC won the first elections in which all citizens were allowed to vote. The long road to freedom had been hard-fought.

CHAPTER FIVE

THE FRENCH IN VIETNAM

Centuries after the conquistadores first made contact with the Incan Empire and long after the British had cemented their hold on India, the French took Vietnam.

The first westerners to live among the Vietnamese were Catholic missionaries. Their presence had been generally peaceful until a rebellion in 1777. Rebels swept the ruling House of Nguyen from power, massacring the entire royal family except for Prince Nguyen Anh. The prince escaped to Phu Quoc Island, where Catholic missionaries urged him to ask the French for help against the new government.

Ho Chi Minh was a committed revolutionary who struggled against France for an independent and united Vietnam.

A Native Backlash

On August 17, 1798, the new ruler, King Canh Thinh, ordered the destruction of all Catholic churches and missions. Persecution lasted until Prince Nguyen was restored as ruler. Remembering the aid given him by the Catholics, he reinstated their freedom of religion.

However, the presence of Catholicism worried many Vietnamese, including Chinese Confucians who struggled against the French in Nguyen's government. The Confucians believed in strictly preserving old traditions.

Nguyen's firstborn son, Prince Canh, had been educated in France. The French hoped that Catholicism would spread during his rule and westernize Vietnam. The Chinese faction supported his younger brother, Prince Mien Tong, who held traditional views.

But French influence soon collapsed. Prince Canh is said to have died from the measles at the age of twenty-one. However, French missionaries reported that he had been poisoned.

Mien Tong was crowned Emperor Minh Mang. Canh's followers were stripped of their powers. Some were executed.

The French Invasion

In France, resentment grew against the anti-Christian attitude in Vietnam. The Vietnamese, cutting off most contact with the world at large, expelled many missionaries from the country. The conservative Confucians resisted change. However, the country stagnated, falling victim to corruption and the breakdown of government.

In 1858, a French expedition landed at Tourane (present-day Danang) requesting permission to set up a consulate and a trading office. When the emperor turned them down, the French took Tourane by force.

The French found a country that was ill-equipped to protect itself. In 1859, France captured the city of Gia Dinh (later known as Saigon and Ho Chi Minh City).

Why did the French want Vietnam? Their motivations were similar to other colonizers. France needed raw materials and markets for its products. Plus, the French felt that their culture was superior to that of Vietnam. They considered it their moral duty to educate people in "unfortunate" regions of the world. Their "refinement" and "humanity" were forced on people at the barrel of a gun.

After a series of battles, the French claimed the areas surrounding Gia Dinh. By June 1862, the Vietnamese emperor, Tu Duc, was forced to sign the Treaty of Saigon.

Tu Duc gave up much of the south, enabling the French to sail their warships up the Mekong River into Cambodia. He also paid the French large sums of money. The French forced neighboring Cambodia to give up some provinces as well.

Soon, the French took the city of Hanoi. Another treaty was forced on Tu Duc in which the Vietnamese emperor was made to concede that the French had "full and entire sovereignty" over North Vietnam.

The capital city of Hue fell in August 1883. Tu Duc himself was not around to see his nation's defeat; he had died a month earlier.

North and central Vietnam now belonged to the French. The new emperor was a figurehead.

How the French Ruled

In 1887, the French created the Indochinese Union. It included South and North Vietnam, central Vietnam, Cambodia, and Laos.

Frenchmen filled all the important government posts. A few Vietnamese officials, left over from the emperor's government, collaborated with the French. However, they had no real power.

Vietnamese who wanted to travel through the country needed to carry identification. The Vietnamese were not allowed freedom of assembly or

This illustration from the nineteenth century shows the French victory over the Vietnamese at Hanoi, which would eventually become the capital of postcolonial Communist North Vietnam.

freedom of the press. French magistrates could imprison people at will. Like other colonized peoples, the Vietnamese were forced to work as unpaid labor, called corvée. By 1925, there were about 5,000 French officials in government posts. They oversaw a native Vietnamese population of about 30 million people.

Economic Conditions Under the French

The French built highways, bridges, canals, and other infrastructure. This helped them to remove vast natural resources including rubber, minerals, and coal. They also exported rice from Vietnam, leaving many Vietnamese to starve.

Some Vietnamese remained landholders under French rule. These included Vietnamese Catholics who collaborated with the French. The lion's share of the land was given to French colonists, called colons. A handful of landlords oversaw a landless peasantry that was so highly taxed it was reduced to poverty. The French also controlled most industry. They owned more than 90 percent of the rubber plantations in Vietnam.

France instituted some reforms to help the native people. However, enforcing them overseas was nearly impossible. Most colonial officials ignored the new rules.

Rebel Movements

Discontent brewed among many Vietnamese. They clung in private to traditional education based on classic Chinese texts. Eventually, anticolonial ideas had begun to surface in their literature.

Though the French controlled the government and exploited Vietnam for its wealth, they could not crush the spirit of the Vietnamese. Resistance leadership, mostly scholars, emerged from the ranks of the old government. One of the most respected men was Phan Boi Chau. A firsthand witness to French oppression, Chau traveled through Vietnam trying to muster the remnants of a rebel movement called the Can Vuoung (which means "Save the King"). Chau believed a nationalist movement could restore the monarchy to Vietnam. In 1904, he formed the Duy Tan Hoi, or the "Reformation Society."

Chau was deported in March 1909 because of his revolutionary activities. As a result, he spent time wandering throughout Asia, preaching resistance from abroad. His efforts against the French grew more desperate. He helped coordinate assassinations and terrorist bombings. The French had him arrested and imprisoned by the Chinese between 1914 and 1917. Later freed, he was kidnapped by French agents in Shanghai, China, to face trial in Hanoi, Vietnam. He died under house arrest in 1940.

A Radicalized Resistance

Another nationalist anticolonial movement rose in 1925 when a young sailor named Nguyen Sinh Cung formed the Revolutionary Youth League of Vietnam. A world traveler, he had become a Communist in Paris. The Communist movement believed that the working people in a country should own all industry and property collectively and share the benefits from them. It sought to do away with what it saw as the evils of capitalism—the rich taking advantage of the poor.

By 1930, Nguyen, later known as Ho Chi Minh (which means "He Who Enlightens"), formed the Indochinese Communist Party. Later, during World War II (1939–1945), the Communist Party joined with other groups to form the Vietminh, or the League for the Independence of Vietnam. After the war, Ho Chi Minh led talks with the French, hoping to secure an independent state. However, the two sides could not

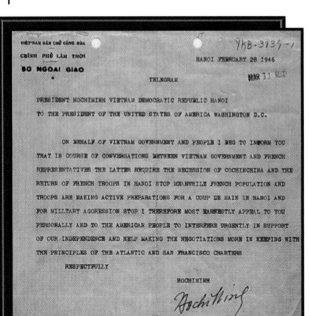

Ho Chi Minh sent this telegram to President Harry Truman on February 28, 1945, seeking Truman's support for the Vietminh's struggle against the French. Refer to page 58 for a transcription of the telegram.

agree. When a French naval attack on the port city of Haiphong killed thousands, the First Indochina War (also called the French Indochina War) began.

The Vietminh Against the French

The Vietminh, led by Ho Chi Minh, fought a guerilla war against the French. When China became Communist in 1949, it, too, aided the Vietnamese Communists. At the time, the United States was embroiled in the Cold War with the Soviet Union, also Communist. It feared what would happen if Vietnam became a Communist nation. Accordingly, the United States supported the French.

The rebels captured a French military garrison at Dien Bien Phu in May 1954. In July 1954, a cease-fire was declared. To reach a settlement, Switzerland, France, and the Democratic Republic of Vietnam met in Geneva. The French were ordered to keep their forces in the south while the Vietminh was allowed to keep its land in the north. National elections were set for July 1956 to decide which direction the country would take.

Ho Chi Minh and the Anticolonial Movement

Born Nguyen Sinh Cung, the man later to be known as Ho Chi Minh was agitating tax revolts when he was a young man. Of humble origins, he deeply resented French colonial rule from an early age.

A cook onboard a French steamship, he moved to Paris, where he joined the French Communist Party. He tried to present a list of French abuses against Vietnam to American president Woodrow Wilson, who was visiting France in 1919.

By 1930, Ho formed the Indochinese Communist Party in Hong Kong. Eventually, he returned home to work against the French.

During World War II, the Japanese invasion of Indochina dealt the French a crippling blow in Vietnam. The Vietminh, which Ho helped form, worked secretly against the Japanese in the region with U.S. help. At the end of the war, with Japan defeated, the Vietminh marched to Hanoi and declared Vietnam independent. The French refused to abdicate their colonial possession, and in 1946, Vietnam was plunged into a war that would last, on and off, for almost thirty years.

The elections never took place. Eventually, the split between the north and south escalated into war again. The United States supported the south once more, while Communist nations fell in with the north. A full decade of war ended in 1975 with the fall of Saigon,

This photograph, taken on November 18, 1950, shows a Communist Vietminh soldier raising his hands in surrender to the French Foreign Legion, a division of the French military that recruits soldiers from all over the world. The legionnaire on the right examines the Vietminh flag, which bears the same hammer and sickle emblem of the Soviet flag.

the capital of the southern government. Millions of Vietnamese died on both sides and more than 50,000 United States soldiers were killed. The long road to Vietnamese reunification was over, and the Communists had prevailed.

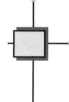

Conclusion: Shadows of the Past

While European colonialism is, in large measure, part of the past, its aftereffects run deep. In 1894, Lord Curzon, the viceroy of British India said, "India is the pivot of our Empire . . . if we lose India, the sun of our Empire will have set." Today historians are looking beyond the age-old myth that colonialism improves the lives of "savages." Instead, many scholars are examining the callous attitudes of colonizers toward the people they colonized.

In India, for example, the British government ignored the growing poverty and hardship of the people whose country they were occupying. Records show that life expectancy for Indians in British India between 1872 and 1931 fell from 55 to 23 years, as Indian lives were dramatically shortened by increased squalor, famine, and disease. Meanwhile, the British were pumping Indian resources, or the profits they earned, into the mother country.

As a result of British colonialism, India's Hindu majority, Muslim minority, and the people of countless other cultures are now linked by speaking English, the language of commerce, science, and of the computer era. However, the British in India ignored the educational needs of the Indian people, creating a pattern of neglect that keeps them struggling today.

In 1911, the literacy rate in British India had been 6 percent. It inched to 8 percent by 1931. By 1935, still only 4 out of 10,000 people attended a university or school of higher education. By 1995, literacy in India had bounced to 52 percent.

In Latin America, most people speak Spanish, share similar cuisine and music, and are members of the Catholic Church. In parts of the Caribbean, the descendants of former slaves have melded old African faiths with the worship of Catholic saints. But millions of lives and many cultures and languages were lost along the way.

The long-term strife created by colonialism can be seen in today's headlines. The nation of Iraq, for example, is not actually a country with a single culture and ethnicity, like a nation such as Poland. Instead, Iraq is a collection of several groups. The majority Shiite Muslims, Sunni Muslims, and Kurds have very little in common with each other. Iraq has existed as a sovereign (independent) nation only since 1932. The British claimed it after the defeat of the Ottoman Empire in World War I (1914–1918).

Racial tensions continue to flare throughout the world in a landscape where colonizers and native people struggle to coexist in a postcolonial reality. On the continent of Africa, new boundaries were created by colonizers for their own convenience. Often, tribes or nations that had been brutal enemies for centuries were forced to live together.

Now, in the postcolonial era, many challenges remain for the former colonies, most of which are part of the developing world. Some nations must reconcile their native roots with European and American influences. Many nations that have formed in the last few decades are struggling over which form of government suits them best. Only time will tell how so many former colonies, now independent nations, will fare in the years to come.

TIMELINE

1492	Christopher Columbus claims the island of Hispaniola for Spain.
1600	Queen Elizabeth I of England grants a charter to the East India Company to run Britain's trade in India.
1607	The first permanent British settlement in North America is established at Jamestown, Virginia.
1619	The first African slaves arrive in Jamestown, Virginia.
1630	Puritans establish the Massachusetts Bay Colony.
1657	Dutch workers begins settling territories in present-day South Africa.
1676	The Bacon Rebellion takes place in Virginia.
1776	The American colonies declare their independence from Britain.
1784	Britain passes the India Act.
1795	Britain invades the Cape region of present-day South Africa.
1835–1843	The Great Trek takes place in present-day South Africa.
1857	The Sepoy Rebellion occurs in India.
1885	The Indian National Congress is formed.
1887	France creates the Indochinese Union.
1899–1902	The Boer War is waged.
1906	The Muslim League is formed in India.
1907	India gains independence from Britain; it is divided into two countries (India and Pakistan).

(Continued on next page)

TIMELINE

1910	The Union of South Africa is established.
1930	Ho Chi Minh forms the Indochinese Communist Party.
1931	South Africa gains independence from Britain.
1944	Nelson Mandela joins the African National Congress in South Africa.
1945–1954	The First Indochina war takes place.
1958	A French expedition captures the Vietnamese city of Tourane.
1964–1975	The Vietnam War is waged.
1994	Nelson Mandela becomes president of South Africa in the nation's first all-race election.

Page 17: PETITION OF THE PEQUOT INDIANS to Governor Joseph Talcott of Connecticut.

Honorable and worthy sir Governor Talcott: We offer our humble respects to your honor. These are to inform you of the wrongs and distress that we meet with by some people who take possession of our land. They destroy so much of our timber for fencing and for other uses that, in a little time, we shall not have enough for fire wood and especially for fencing. We find it is in vain to plant within their enclosures because we planted there last spring and our corn was destroyed by the English creatures. By fencing in of our land, they take away in a great measure the privilege of our orchards for they let their own swines go in and eat up our apples and bed down. If our swines accidentally get in, they commit them to the pound, which we could not subsist without keeping some creatures. We should be glad if we could have more of the produce of the land to keep other creatures.

Also, they removed a great part of our general field to erect their own fence which is greatly to our damage, for some of it had been planted but two years and the English build housing upon our land and put tenants in them. One of them [uses] our apples in making cider, and for other use, and they sow wheat upon our land. Inasmuch as we see plainly that their primary desire is to deprive us of the privilege of our land, and drive us off to our utter ruin, it makes us concerned for our children. What will become of them, for they are about having the gospel preached to them, and are learning to read, and all our young men and women that are capable of learning of it. Some of our young men would be glad to build housing on it, and live as the English do. Could they have a sufficiency of the produce of the land? We crave your patience, and we will acquaint you a little further. The other of their tenants puts cattle at night into our general field among our corn and take them out in the morning. And when we tell them to take care and keep out their creatures they threaten us if we don't hold our tongues to beat our brains out. He threatens us that we shall not plant there another year. Also, some people cut our stalks some time when the corn is in the milk. We should be glad if there could be a stop put to it. The stalks beings our own labor, we should be glad to have them for our own use, for we find that we can't very well subsist without keeping some creatures. We should be very thankful if there could be some ways found out and thought of wherein our land and the privilege thereof be restored to us again. I think we have given your honor a true account as near as our memory serves, but a great deal might be added. But we would not be too tedious to your honor and so we remain your servants to command.

Page 22: Olive Branch Petition (excerpt)

MOST GRACIOUS SOVEREIGN: We, your Majesty's faithful subjects of the Colonies of New-Hampshire, Massachusetts-Bay, Rhode-Island, New-Jersey, Pennsylvania, the Counties of Newcastle, Kent, and Sussex, on Delaware, Maryland, Virginia, North Carolina, and South Carolina, in behalf of ourselves and the inhabitants of these Colonies, who have deputed us to represent them in General Congress, entreat your Majesty's gracious attention to this our humble petition . . .

Attached to your Majesty's person, family, and Government, with all devotion that principle and affection can inspire; connected with Great Britain by the strongest ties that can unite societies, and deploring every event that tends in any degree to weaken them, we solemnly assure your

Majesty, that we not only most ardently desire the former harmony between her and these Colonies may be restored, but that a concord may be established between them upon so firm a basis as to perpetuate its blessings, uninterrupted by any future dissensions, to succeeding generations in both countries, and to transmit your Majesty's name to posterity, adorned with that signal and lasting glory that has attended the memory of those illustrious personages, whose virtues and abilities have extricated states from dangerous convulsions, and by securing the happiness to others, have erected the most noble and durable monuments to their own fame.

We beg further leave to assure your Majesty, that notwithstanding the sufferings of your loyal Colonists during the course of this present controversy, our breasts retain too tender a regard for the kingdom from which we derive our origin, to request such a reconciliation as might, in any manner, be inconsistent with her dignity or welfare. These, related as we are to her, honour and duty, as well as inclination, induce us to support and advance; and the apprehensions that now oppress our hearts with unspeakable grief, being once removed, your Majesty will find our faithful subject on this Continent ready and willing at all times, as they have ever been with their lives and fortunes, to assert and maintain the rights and interests of your Majesty, and of our Mother Country.

We therefore beseech your Majesty, that your royal authority and influence may be graciously interposed to procure us relief from our afflicting fears and jealousies, occasioned by the system before-mentioned, and to settle peace through every part of our Dominions, with all humility submitting to your Majesty's wise consideration, whether it may not be expedient, for facilitating thoseimportant purposes, that your Majesty be pleased to direct some mode, by which the united applications of your faithful Colonists to the Throne, in pursuance of their common counsels, may be improved into a happy and permanent reconciliation; and that, in the mean time, measures may be taken for preventing the further destruction of the lives of your Majesty's subjects; and that such statutes as more immediately distress any of your Majesty's Colonies may be repealed.

For such arrangements as your Majesty's wisdom can form for collecting the united sense of your American people, we are convinced your Majesty would receive such satisfactory proofs of the disposition of the Colonists towards their Sovereign and Parent State, that the wished for opportunity would soon be restored to them, of evincing the sincerity of their professions, by every testimony of devotion becoming the most dutiful subjects, and the most affectionate Colonists.

That your Majesty may enjoy long and prosperous reign, and that your descendants may govern your Dominions with honour to themselves and happiness to their subjects, is our sincere prayer.

Page 50: February 28, 1946, Telegram from Ho Chi Minh to President Truman

On behalf of Vietnam government and people I beg to inform you that in course of conversations between Vietnam government and French representatives the latter require the secession of Cochinchina and the return of French troops in Hanoi. Meanwhile French population and troops are making active preparations for a coup de main in Hanoi and for military agression. I therefore most earnestly appeal to you personally and to the American people to interfere urgently in support of our independence and help making the negotiations more in keeping with principles of the Atlantic and San Francisco charters.

GLOSSARY

colony A territory that has been settled by people from another country and is controlled by that country.

colonialism An economic, social, and political system that existed from the fifteenth to the twentieth centuries in which colonies were used by conquering nations as sources of economic and military advantage

conquistador The Spanish word for "conqueror." The conquistadores were the Spanish explorers and conquerors of much of Central and South America starting in the fifteenth century.

encomienda A piece of land in Spain's colonies in the New World, controlled by a Spaniard who had power over any native people that lived on that land.

Hinduism The dominant religion in India.

Inca A people native to South America whose empire, based in modern-day Peru, was conquered by the Spanish in the sixteenth century.

Indian A term used to refer to either the people native to the nation of India or to the indigenous people of North and South America who were conquered by Europeans starting in the sixteenth century.

Islam The religious faith of Muslims including belief in Allah as the sole deity and Muhammad as his prophet; the group of modern nations in which Islam is the dominant religion.

Mughals A Muslim people that ruled much of India before the British took over.

nawab An Indian prince.

zamindar A tax collector in Bengal prior to British rule.

FOR MORE INFORMATION

Due to the changing nature of Internet links, the Rosen Publishing Group, Inc., has developed an online list of Web sites related to the subject of this book. This site is updated regularly. Please use this link to access the list:

http://www.rosenlinks.com/psps/colo

FOR FURTHER READING

Baquedano , Elizabeth. Aztec, Inca, and Maya. New York: DK Publishing, 2000.

Chatterjee, Manini, and Anita Roy. Eyewitness: India (Eyewitness Books). New York: DK Publishing, 2002.

Goalen, Paul. India: From Mughal Empire to British Raj. Cambridge, England: Cambridge University Press, 1993.

Kalman, Bobby. Vietnam: The People (Lands, Peoples, and Cultures). New York: Crabtree Publishing, 2002.

Lace, William W. The British Empire: The End of Colonialism (History's Great Defeats). San Diego: Lucent Books, 2000.

Severance, John B. Gandhi, Great Soul. Boston: Houghton Mifflin Company, 1997.

Worth, Richard. Pizarro and the Conquest of the Incan Empire in World History. Berkeley Heights, NJ: Enslow Publishers, 2000.

Yamasaki, Mitch. Vietnam War: How the United States Became Involved. Carlisle, MA: Discovery Enterprises, Ltd., 1997.

BIBLIOGRAPHY

Césaire, Aimé. Discourse on Colonialism. New York: Monthly Review Press, 1972.

Curtin, Philip D. The World and the West: The European Challenge and the Overseas Response in the Age of Empire. Cambridge, England: Cambridge University Press, 2000.

Kiernan, V. G. The Lords of Human Kind: Black Man, Yellow Man, and White Man in an Age of Empire. Boston: Little, Brown and Company, 1969.

Marshall, P. J., ed. The Cambridge Illustrated History of the British Empire. Cambridge, England: Cambridge University Press, 1996.

Osterhammel, Jürgen. Colonialism: A Theoretical Overview. Princeton, NJ: Markus Wiener Publishers, 1997.

Sowell, Thomas. Conquests and Cultures: An International History. New York: Basic Books, 1999.

Page 9: Engraving portraying the strangulation of Atahuallpa by Francisco Pizarro's soldiers, 1595.

Page 17: Petition of the Pequot Indians to Governor Joseph Talcott of Connecticut, September 22, 1735.

Page 22: The Olive Branch Petition, July 5, 1775. Housed at the National Archives in Washington, D.C.

Page 23: Portrait of Queen Victoria, 1886, by Alexander Bassano.

Page 27: "Pitt and Napoléon Divide the World," political cartoon by James Gillray, 1809.

Page 31: Photograph of Lord Curzon, 1895.

Page 32: Photograph of Mohandas Ghandi, 1941

Page 33: Photograph of Lord Louis Mountbatten announcing Indian Independence on August 15, 1947.

Page 34: Photograph of Baron Horatio Kitchener, circa 1890s.

Page 37: Wanted poster for the capture of Winston Churchill.

Page 42: Photograph of Nelson Mandela at a press conference in Cape Town, South Africa, in May 1990.

Page 44: Photograph of Ho Chi Minh at a press conference in Sophia, Bulgaria, on August 13, 1957.

Page 47: Nineteenth-century illustration depicting the capture of Hanoi by French forces.

Page 50: February 28, 1946, telegram from Ho Chi Minh to President Harry Truman.

Page 52: Associated Press photograph showing a Vietminh fighter surrendering to French forces in Vietnam in 1950.

INDEX

A

African National Congress (ANC), 41, 42, 43
Africans, 11, 19, 22, 34–43
Age of Exploration, 5–6
American Revolution, 22
apartheid, 37, 39, 41, 42, 43
Aztecs, 10

B

Bacon's Rebellion, 19–20
Black Hole of Calcutta, 24–25
Boers, 35, 36–39

C

Caribbean, 7
Catholicism/Catholics, 10, 45, 48, 53, 54
Chau, Phan Boi, 48–49
Clive, Robert, 24, 26
Columbus, Christopher, 7
Communism, 49, 51, 52
Cornwallis, Charles, 27–28
Curzon, Lord George N., 31, 53

D

de la Gasca, Pedro, 13
disease/illness, 8, 11, 15, 19, 20
Dutch East India Company, 34

E

East India Company, 24, 25, 26, 27, 30
Elizabeth of England, Queen, 24
encomienda system, 10–11, 13

F

Fort Stanwix, Treaty of, 18

G

Gandhi, Mohandas, 32

H

Ho Chi Minh, 49, 50, 51

I

Incas, 8, 10, 12, 44
indentured servants, 15, 20
India
    Britain and, 6, 23–33, 44, 53
    independence of, 30–33
    India Act, 26
Indian National Congress (INC), 30–31
Indochina, 6
Indochinese Union, 47
Industrial Revolution, 23
Inter Caetera, 9–10
Iraq, 54
Iroquois League, 18

J

Jamestown, 15, 19–20

M

Mandela, Nelson, 42, 43
missions/missionaries, 11, 44, 45
Mughals, 24

N

Native Americans, 10–11, 13, 14, 15, 17, 18, 19–20, 21, 22
New Laws (Spain), 11, 13
New World, the
    Britain and the, 14–22
    Spain and the, 7–13
Nguyen, Prince Anh, 44, 45

P

Pan-Africanist Congress (PAC), 43
Parliament, British, 26, 40, 41
Pequot Indians, 16, 17
Pilgrims, 15–17
Pitt, William, 26
Pizarro, Francisco, 8, 13
Pizarro, Gonzalo, 13

COLONIALISM: A Primary Source Analysis

plantation system, 21
Plymouth colony, 15–17
Portugal, 8, 10

R
Regulating Act of 1773, 26
religion, 15, 17, 45
Roman Catholic Church, 9

S
Saigon, Treaty of, 46
Sepoy Rebellion, 28–30
Siraj-ud-Dawlah, Nawab, 24–25
slaves/slavery, 10, 11, 14, 15, 19, 20,
    21, 22, 35, 36, 54
Sobukwe, Robert, 43
South Africa
    British in, 36, 37–39
    Dutch in, 34–43
subsidiary system, 26

U
United States, 5, 50, 51

V
Vietminh, 49, 50, 51
Vietnam
    French invasion of, 6, 44–47
    French rule of, 47–48
    resistance, 48–52
Virginia House of Burgesss, 19–20

W
Wampanoag, 17, 19
Wellesley, Lord Richard
    Colley, 26
World War I, 54
World War II,

Z
zamindars (India), 28

PHOTO CREDITS

Cover, pp. 1 (right), 27, 31, 38, 40 © Hulton-Deutsch Collection/Corbis; back cover (top left) NARA; back cover (all others) © The 2000 Nova Corporation; pp. 1 (top left), 23 © Gianni Dagli Orti/Corbis; pp. 1 (bottom), 25, 32, 37 © Hulton/Archive/ Getty Images; pp. 4–5, 9, 16, 29, 33, 34, 47 © Bettmann/Corbis; p. 7 © The Art Archive/Musée du Château de Versailles/Dagli Orti; p. 12 © Christie's Images/ Corbis; p. 14 Washington-Curtis-Lee Collection, Washington and Lee University, VA; pp. 17, 22 © MPI/Hulton/Archive/Getty Images; p. 42 © Louise Gubb/Corbis Saba; pp. 44, 52 © AP/Wide World Photos; p. 50 © NARA.

ABOUT THE AUTHOR
Philip Wolny is a freelance writer and editor who lives in Los Angeles, California.

Designer: Nelson Sá; **Editor:** Wayne Anderson;
Photo Researcher: Hillary Arnold